# Summer of Change
Martha Passel

One of the darkest moments of my life may have been the morning I awoke and found PerryAnn was gone. I was in the middle of a dream; I was an Indian princess. We were breaking camp to move high into the mountains for the winter when I heard a loud thud that awakened me. I opened my eyes and was about to give PerryAnn a glare for the noise, but there was no PerryAnn and no visible reason for the sound. It was 1973; it was the year I was eleven. Just three months before, she had arrived at the farm across the field from ours on one of the hottest days of the summer, and now she was gone.

# CHAPTER ONE

We'd moved to our farm when I was six. "Mary, do we want to live our remaining years here in the city or get back to New Mexico?" my father asked my mother one day. A picture of them, taken the summer they'd met, stared at me from the bookshelf as I heard him ask. He was covered with dirt, a shovel in hand, and stood stocky with red curly hair, freckles, and green eyes. She towered beside him stoic like a tree, her dark eyes peering out of the frame, and her long black hair blown by the wind. A month later he landed a position to teach geology at the university in Albuquerque. He had come barreling through the front door.

"What do you girls think about going to New Mexico?"

"Mike Butler, don't tease me," my mother squealed.

"I'm not, Mary. I found a job and a farm to buy. Seriously."

"Yes," she smiled as her teeth peeked out from behind her parted lips. My father took her hand and mine in his, twirled us around, and we all screamed together.

When he bought the farm, I heard my father tell the man on the phone, "I won't buy unless it comes with the mineral rights." I didn't understand what it meant. I was only six. "What's that mean?" I asked. He took a piece of paper and drew a line across the page. On top of the line he drew a barn and wrote farm. Below it he drew pictures of worms and rocks and wrote the words 'dirt and minerals.' I still have the paper in my drawer.

My eyes are green; my skin is fair and freckled like my father. I may have dreamed I was an Indian princess the morning PerryAnn disappeared, but I didn't resemble one. Both she and my mother looked like they had Indian blood in their veins with their olive skin, dark hair and eyes, and they were both tall. I was short. If you stood all three of us side by side, you'd think they belonged together and I was from another tribe.

Life was fun on our farm in those five years before PerryAnn arrived. I ran through fields that stretched as far as you could see. The air was clean; you could smell the rain. No wire fences, no concrete roads and no piles of rusty equipment cluttered our forty acres. And there were plenty of deer, wild turkeys, hogs, raccoons, skunks, squirrels and rabbits to chase. When the sun rose and set, there wasn't any haze of smoke, only clouds and sky. I'd lie on my back in the grass for hours and look up, or climb the big oak near the woodshed, or hike the small foothills. The creek was a favorite spot to search for tadpoles. It ran behind the barn to the road and down through the cemetery. Every now and then, I read the headstones there. It was creepy.

We called it a farm, but really it wasn't. We did have our vegetable garden in back and sometimes we'd take the surplus vegetables to the Saturday farmers' market near the

Indian reservation. Twice a week my father drove fifty miles to Albuquerque to teach his class. When he was gone, my mother spent hours painting landscapes. Our land was three miles from town. "Why don't you invite someone from school out here to play?" my mother would ask. I did wish for a friend, but the girls in my class lived in town and told me, "It's too far to come out there." I didn't care. Most of them were mean anyway. One day I asked my father, "Why don't I have a brother or sister?" He picked me up and swung me around by my arms. "Lucky girl, you have all our love for yourself."

I'd pretend to be a scientist like my father and study nature around me. For an interesting 'people we know' assignment, he came to class and talked about his expedition to Antarctica. My father told us about studies where he'd measured the amount of time it took his face to freeze in different wind conditions. He brought slides of Admiral Byrd, Antarctic rocks, penguins and snow drifts thirty feet high. It was cool, and I was a rock star that day. I mean I was popular, with the boys mostly, for having him there. When I went to the bathroom, the meanest girl in class sneered, "Baby had to ask her daddy for show and tell."

Rocks weren't my interest, but creatures, all of them, were. My happiest days were observing wildlife. I'd seen my father's charts from experiments in Antarctica. "How long did it take to freeze?" I asked him once. *It must be really cold to freeze your face.* My experiments weren't as neat, but I had tried to make my charts look like his. When he'd review them, he'd look over the rim of his glasses and say, "MatiLou, did you consider the season, the date, time, and weather?" Often I hadn't, but he'd still say, "You're my smart girl." Maybe it was because I'd made the highest marks on IQ testing at our school. The teacher had told my parents my scores were nearly genius. I don't feel like a genius, but I do wander around in my thinking and speech. Maybe that's why I scored so high.

I remember when my father caught me hanging upside down from a limb in the oak tree behind the barn. I was observing hatchlings below me, and my face was only a few feet from the nest. He scolded me that night. "Keep your distance." He told me wildlife biologists study creatures. "They're careful not to disturb the subjects or their habitat. You should act like that when you do your research," he said. After that, when a baby squirrel fell from a tree, I waited three hours, keeping my distance, to see if the mama would come for it. It was all I could do to sit still and wait. I whispered over and over, "It's okay little baby squirrel," until my mother finally yelled out the back door, "Matilda Louise, what are you doing? Come in here right now." *I told her MatiLou's what I like.* When I snuck out an hour later, the mama had the baby in her mouth and was heading up the tree.

The day PerryAnn arrived, in the summer of 1973, I was sitting in a tree near the road. A VW bus pulled up to the mailbox and stopped. As Grandma Waters emerged in a flowered dress from her house and stood by the drive, a girl jumped out of the van. The driver saw her and left the girl by the mailbox. He turned in and drove halfway to where Grandma Waters stood and yelled through the open window, "We should be back from Oklahoma in three weeks." The man looked like an Indian warrior to me. The gear clunked into reverse, and he backed out the drive.

"Don't give Grandma any trouble," I heard the light skinned woman sitting beside him yell to the girl. I jumped out of the tree and headed across the field to where she stood by the mailbox on the road. *Who is she? This girl reminds me of pictures of Pocahontas.*

When I reached her, she was watching the van climb the hill and vanish from view. "Hey, I am MatiLou. I live over there." I pointed to our farm. "Who are they?" I asked.

"My parents," the girl said.

"Why'd they drop you off out here by the road?" I asked.

"Heck if I know. I think they're in a hurry."

"Meow." A tabby cat peeked out of the cloth carrying case sitting on the ground by her feet.

"By the way, that's Spanky. I'm PerryAnn."

She reached for her bag and started walking down the drive. "Can you grab Spanky?" I picked up the case and walked with her.

When I got closer to Grandma Waters, she glared at me. I'd seen that look. "No chasing rabbits, girl!" she screeched. A long braid cascaded down her back like a waterfall until it reached the tops of her legs. I hadn't seen the braid unwrapped in a long while. It was coiled like a small garden snake on top of her head the last time I'd stepped onto her farm three months before. I'd chased a rabbit into her cactus garden after my mother announced I could keep one if I could catch it. My father chimed in he'd build a hutch and maybe we'd breed babies for sale. I thought it was weird since he'd told me to keep my distance from the wildlife, but it didn't stop me from trying. Anyway, when Grandma Waters saw me chasing the rabbit with my net that day, she grabbed my arm, pierced me with her dark eyes and yelled, "Girl, leave it be!" The deep grooves in her face and dark spaces where teeth once lined her smile seemed to jump out at me. I hadn't set foot on her farm again until PerryAnn appeared that morning.

# CHAPTER TWO

It looked like PerryAnn just might be the answer to my wish for a friend. The next day we walked three miles on railroad tracks to the general store where we ordered hamburgers and sodas. Her parents had left money with her to spend, and I raided my piggy bank, the coins I saved doing dishes after dinner, so I could go. Afterward, we looked through the clothes racks, tapes and books at the adjacent thrift store. And when we finished doing all that, we went to the bowling alley.

We did the same thing every day for the next three weeks. Sometimes we went to the dollar cinema, but on afternoons we saw PG rated movies, I told my mother we'd gone to the bowling alley instead.

We were whistled at in those days we went to town more than I'd been the whole rest of my eleven years. I figured they were really whistling at PerryAnn, since I'd only be twelve on December 23rd. Having a birthday so close to Christmas is yucky. Every year we celebrate my birthday at the Christmas Eve dinner. *Why can't we just celebrate on the day I was born?*

When we returned from our outing into town at the end of the third week, Spanky was sitting in the windowsill with a questioning look like he was waiting for a report on our whereabouts. "PerryAnn, let's do something outside tomorrow!" I blurted as we passed by his post and opened the front door. I was bored with going to town every day and wanted to explore the creek or do anything outdoors, but she was more interested in the town. Even though it was small, it was where she wanted to go every single afternoon.

"No, I want to go to town again," she said.

"Figures," I muttered.

"Hey did you see the boy in the back of the white truck we passed when we turned down the tracks?" she asked.

"I saw him, but he looked too old for you. Why?" I'd only know her a few weeks, but PerryAnn seemed boy crazy to me. She wouldn't even be fifteen until March.

"Just wondered," she said and looked at Spanky. "You're a bad cat. You got on the roof again!" she said and looked at me. "He howled for an hour." She picked Spanky up. "Didn't you?" she said to him. "You're lucky Grandma didn't hear you."

"What'd he do that for?" I asked.

"Only he knows. It wasn't the first time either. He used to get up on my parent's roof and howl and howl. The first time he did it, I freaked out and called the fire department. The fireman put a ladder up to bring him down and as soon as the fire truck was gone, he went to the back of the house, climbed the trellis and went to the same spot."

"He's weird," I said.

"I know," PerryAnn acknowledged. "The next time I got a ladder, and then I figured out that he'd come down on his own. Since we been here, he's climbed the roof three times. I can't figure out how he's getting up there. He isn't allowed outside. There must be a hole inside somewhere."

"Meow." He'd jumped down and was rubbing her leg with his tail.

We were in PerryAnn's room a few days later when she heard Grandma Waters tell the principal, Mr. Holmes, to enroll her in seventh grade in September. PerryAnn bolted into the hall as Grandma Waters placed the receiver on the hook. "Why am I staying here? Mom and Dad are supposed to pick me up next week. Why aren't they coming back?"

Grandma Waters peered at me. "Go home, MatiLou."
*Why didn't she invite me to stay tonight? Is she mad?*

Coyotes barked as I crossed the field. An owl hooted in the distance. The stars seemed brighter than I'd ever seen them when the moon was full. I had an eerie feeling in my stomach, but I didn't know quite why. It was like a stomachache from too much cotton candy.

When I got home my dad told me PerryAnn's father had fallen asleep at the wheel. His VW bus had veered into the oncoming lane and over the side of the road into the ravine. Both her mother and her father had been killed.

The next morning, when I crossed the field, a crow circled overhead. I walked into Grandma Waters' living room where PerryAnn sat in a trance staring through the front window. She jumped up and burst through the screen door as I opened it.

"Wait," I called after her.

"Leave her be," Grandma Waters said as she grabbed my arm and pulled me back.

I looked through the screen door, and a man in uniform was walking up the drive and passed by PerryAnn. He stepped onto the porch and knocked on the screen. Under the name on his shirt were the words Tribal Police Chief. "Why are you here instead of the regular police?" Grandma Waters asked. She seemed to know him. He explained to her the accident had happened on a strip of road within the reservation. It was in the tribal police jurisdiction, he said. "Here's the accident report and a note we found in the van. I'm sorry about Perry. He was a good man." He cleared his throat. "The bodies are at the city morgue until you are ready to bury them." He handed two pieces of paper to her. It seemed cold to me.

That evening, the note and accident report were lying on the kitchen table in front of PerryAnn. She sat like a stone in the chair with her elbows folded on the table. I peeked at both pieces of paper as I pulled out a chair to sit down. The report said the accident was no fault. The note read, "Bury me in New Mexico under tree in field with mountain." I wasn't sure, but I guessed the note was from her mother. It looked like she started to write 'view,' but the word trailed off the page in a thin line made by the pen.

Both papers sat on the table like they had no more importance than a grocery list or a recipe. I could hear the creak of the walls as the wind blew hard outside. Grandma Waters stood at the kitchen sink staring out the window with her back to us. "I wish my son could be high on stilts in sacred burial ground on the reservation like ancestors," she said under her breath.

"Grandma, it's 1973. There are no stilts or bodies lying on top out there anymore. There haven't been for years. That's stupid."

She turned to face PerryAnn. "Where you wish graves to be?"

"I guess together, Grandma. You said Mom's parents want her buried in the cemetery, I guess Dad could be there, too? I heard you on the phone with Mom's mother yesterday. I want to stay here with you. Please, I don't want to live in Oklahoma."

That morning while I sat at the kitchen table with them, Grandma Waters and PerryAnn agreed to bury her parents in the cemetery, instead of the sacred Indian burial grounds. Perry's tribal name, Walking in the Cloud, wouldn't be on the headstone. Instead, the tombstones would read Perry and Ann Waters.

When my mother and I went to the general store the day before the funeral, we overheard a woman talking on the phone. "It was hard when Ann married Perry," she said. "No, she did not return to the university to finish her archeology degree. It has been strained... Yes, they want a Christian burial. The tribal elders will perform rites, too."

The day of the burial, PerryAnn wore a black dress with thin white vertical stripes. Her hair was piled on top of her head, but not neatly. She stood as still as the oak tree offering its shade while the preacher read the eulogies.

"Perry and Ann Waters met when he conducted tours on the reservation for outsiders to see how Indian ancestors lived. The elders say their eyes locked with the powers of lightning. PerryAnn was born nine months and three weeks after they married. There are no mistakes in God's plan."

*What? What about the accident? Is he saying it wasn't a mistake?*

There was a pause and the preacher continued. "Ann came from a Christian background, Perry from Native American, and there were problems between the families through the years. We need to put those differences behind, for the sake of PerryAnn standing before us." He looked directly at Ann's parents as he said it.

Ann's mother and father looked down as the coffins were lowered into the ground, and I watched as PerryAnn looked up at the clouds. She glanced briefly at the estranged parents of her mother. When I caught her eye, I mouthed, "Are you okay?" She nodded, but looked away. The only sounds were dirt hitting the coffin lids and a group of squirrels squabbling in the tree overhead.

As the last dirt was shoveled into the graves, Jim, the attorney from Albuquerque, who worked with her father, and his wife, Betty, stepped up and gave PerryAnn a hug. The graying hair around Jim's temples blended with the gray suit he wore and Betty's eyes matched the color of her green dress. I knew who they were because PerryAnn had told me about them when we'd walk on the railroad tracks to town. PerryAnn's parents, now laid to rest, side by side, under the same kind of oak tree where I'd observed the mama squirrel rescue her baby that had fallen from the nest. I felt a knot in my stomach when I looked at the graves as the last dirt was piled on top.

The next morning, I sat behind our barn hoping to catch a rabbit. I thought about the accident, the papers I'd seen on the kitchen table and the service. I wondered about her parents, Perry and Ann, lying in their coffins underground. I looked over, saw Grandma Waters outside watering her cactus, and walked across the field to where she stood. Everyone called her Grandma Waters, but her full tribal name was Waters Running Fast. PerryAnn had told me it was said she would glide on the current of swollen streams after it rained, with her legs and arms outstretched, when she was a girl.

"I was wondering how PerryAnn got her name." I said.

She didn't look up and continued to water. I thought she hadn't heard me, but after a few moments she spoke. "Her mother wanted to name her traditional white name, but Perry wanted her to have tribal name. They couldn't agree, so they named her PerryAnn after themselves."

"But Perry is a white name," I said.

"I changed his name to Perry when he was a boy. Easier to have... His tribal name was 'Walking in the Cloud.' My son wanted to name PerryAnn 'Cloud.'"

"|Cloud's pretty." She looked so heavy as I said it; I thought she'd fall in a heap in the middle of her cactus garden.

When I got home, I asked my father why I had my name. He told me I was named after my grandmothers,

Matilda and Louise. "Old fashioned. I don't like it," I said to him.

"You like MatiLou, don't you?"

"Yeah, I guess it's ok," I replied. The same day I asked him about my name, I happened upon a note in my mother's drawer. Her desk was off limits, but I was looking for a magnifying glass for one of my experiments. The note said "Dear Baby Matilda Louise," and below it were the words "I can't bear the pain." I asked my father what it meant. It was then he told me that two years before I was born, my mother lost a child she was carrying. The day she lost the baby girl was in March. He told me not to speak of it to her.

*"Is she angry with me?"*

I wondered: If Baby Matilda Louise had lived, would I have even been born?

It was a weird thought.

# CHAPTER THREE

A few days after I found the note in my mother's desk drawer, I ran across the field to Grandma Waters. PerryAnn was in bed with her back to me when I entered the room. I told her about the note I'd found in my mother's drawer, but she didn't say a word and just lay there staring through the window at the clouds. "Come on, let's go to the general store and the cinema. They changed the movie yesterday. Let's see what's there," I pleaded, but she wouldn't budge. I was tired of trying to get her out of the bed. I felt the blood rushing to my ears. I wanted to scream at her.

"So, PerryAnn, we're named for people who are dead. It's weird. We can start a club where you have to be named for the dead before you can belong," I blurted. I hadn't told her yet that I was named for my two dead grandmothers. She rolled over so fast I thought she might fall off the bed, looked at me and burst out crying. It was the first time I'd seen her cry.

"Get out!" she screamed.

I vowed that was last time I'd call her PerryAnn to her face. I would think of a nickname to call her from that day on.

"Okay, I'm sorry." I was so mad, but felt bad I'd made her cry. I left her room and went to the kitchen. "Can I have some lemonade?" Grandma Waters handed me a glass.

"Where were they going?" I asked

"Who?" she replied.

"Where were PerryAnn's parents going when they ran off the road?" I stirred two spoons of sugar into my glass.

"Over to Oklahoma." she sighed.

"Why?"

"*Natives for Nature*. They were going to a rally," she replied.

"Why were they going to the rally? What's Natives for Nature?"

"They were fighting drilling. Going to speak."

"Why?" I asked again.

"You're smart girl. I tell you," she replied in her broken English. I'd told PerryAnn, I got the highest score on the IQ test. *Did she tell Grandma Waters?*

She cleared her throat. "My ancestors lived here for many moons. Our people see harm to land and creatures. My son felt purpose to fight for beauty we lived in all our years here."

I'd seen the yards with tanks near the Indian Reservation. Wells, which stood like men on a chessboard, were next to the ancient sacred burial grounds, where Grandma Waters said PerryAnn's ancestors lay at rest. My mother complained the landscape had changed so much; it was hard for her to find an unspoiled view of the mountains to paint. Equipment yards, pumps, large tanks, pits that stank like something rotten was in them and dirt roads now cluttered once pristine fields.

"My son was making a difference. He was getting attention. Government sent a letter saying agency will send men. They were getting noticed. Jim Moate was helping," Grandma Waters said.

"I hope we never have the pits with stagnant water, oil, and green slime close to where we live," I said. "I wish I'd lived with the Indians."

Grandma Waters sighed and started to chop onions. She was making soup.

"The way they are doing drilling is bad for nature. They clear ancestors' land, so few men line pockets." Her dark eyes grew large as she spoke. The braid on top of her head looked more like a small sleeping kitten than a coiled snake ready to strike. A lump formed in my throat and my eyes filled with water as I listened to Grandma Waters speak.

*Where will the creatures, the squirrels, and rabbits live if lands are cleared near here?*

The next thing that happened was weird. A man knocked on the door to ask if Grandma Waters wanted to lease her minerals rights. *We were just talking about that.* "Hello ma'am, my name is Joe. I am here to see if you would like to lease your land."

"No," she said. "No well on my land! My son told me you can put well on my land if I lease."

As he put his hand on the screen handle, he said, "The company taking the lease is drilling thirty miles away, but they don't think the trend is this way. They probably won't drill here, but they want to take a lease so other companies won't either. It would protect you. If you have a minute, I will tell you what the payment will be if you lease. May I come in?"

"Well…okay," Grandma Waters said. She opened the screen and let him in the house.

I was struck dumb by his looks as I sat on the couch and listened to his spiel. He reminded me of a movie star with his blond hair and blue eyes.

Joe began. "Let me first say that if you sell the minerals rights, you will get a lot more than the amount I am going to tell you next. I can pay you four thousand dollars if you lease. You'll only receive additional money if a well is drilled and produces. There is no guarantee on that. Like I said, the company isn't looking at drilling here. They just want the acreage for protection, so another company won't lease it."

"Okay, I don't want a well near here. My son fought drilling for *Natives for Nature*. He's dead. I used all my money to bury him."

*I wonder why they need a protection lease if they aren't going to drill.* Grandma Waters didn't ask the question.

Joe was about to say something when she asked, "How much if I sell?" *What is she doing? We were just talking about it.* PerryAnn peeked out of her room to see who was there, saw Joe sitting with his back to her on the couch and closed her door.

I jumped up to go get her, but then Joe said, "I'm sorry about your son, ma'am. Maybe the money you'd get if you sell will help with your expense. It'll be four times as much or sixteen thousand dollars. Like I said, there is only a small chance there would be a well close to your farm because geology doesn't support drilling wells near here. The company man told my boss that."

When Joe left twenty minutes later, PerryAnn came out of her room. She was dressed and her hair was combed. "Where's the man? Who was he, Grandma?"

"I sold him minerals under the farm. Now I have money to buy things I need. I didn't go to school, but now I have money for you," Grandma said.

"Grandma! That was fast. How'd you do that so fast? What does it mean? Dad didn't want anything to do with those people."

"I know, but he said they won't drill near the farm. He said his boss approves what he turns in. I believe he tells the truth about no well near the farm. It's sixteen thousand dollars," Grandma replied.

"Did you sign anything?" PerryAnn asked. "You should've called someone, Grandma. I don't trust them."

"Yes, I signed a paper called 'deed.' He says he'd have a lady to put something called notary on and will bring me copy. He's coming with check tomorrow."

The next night around supper, the doorbell rang. Joe was at our door. I overheard him tell the same story to my dad about what he would pay to lease or buy our mineral rights. Dad asked if he could see the geology, but Joe told him it belonged to the company. He said it was confidential who they were. *Why was it a secret?* He didn't have the information, he said. As he made his offer, my father said no to the lease and no to the sale of our minerals rights. Before he stepped off the porch, Dad asked Joe if any of the neighbors had signed.

"The lady over there signed yesterday," he replied. He pointed to Grandma Waters' cactus farm.

My father called Grandma Waters as soon as Joe left. "That young man dropped a copy of signed deed by an hour ago. He showed me book and page at top. He say it was public record now... for my protection."

"Why didn't you call me before you signed?" my father questioned her.

"He says no drilling 'round here. I can use cash he offered me," she said.

"She was drunk and slurring her words," my father told my mother as he put the receiver in its hook.

"Mary, get on the phone tomorrow and call the paper to place an ad for a meeting at the town hall. Start calling the neighbors within five miles. We need to make sure everyone understands what is happening with the leasing." My mother got the phone book, paper, and a pen.

"Let's see, the farms are forty acres each mostly. Some are eighty acres, one hundred sixty or more, but most are forty," she muttered to herself as she wrote the names on the list.

Now it seemed my father was to step into the shoes that PerryAnn's father had worn, and we were in a fight to preserve our land; but as it turned out, it was too late. All the surrounding farms were already leased by the time my father had been approached.

What we didn't know at the time was larger farms surrounding Grandma Waters and ours had leased, but in their leases they included language that there would be no well located on their land. So, all the surrounding farms were leased, but no well could be placed on their lands. Our unleased farm and Grandma Waters forty mineral acres she'd sold – were in the middle of it all.

A few weeks before the day PerryAnn disappeared, they came to stake the land for a well on Grandma Waters' cactus farm. The colors on the desert floor were bright orange and green from the sun's midmorning reflection when a white truck pulled up the drive.

Grandma Waters was standing in the yard watering her cactus in the same flowered dress she'd worn the day PerryAnn had arrived. The logo on the side of the truck in large black letters spelled, "RW Surveying Company." PerryAnn and I were sitting on the front porch swing sipping fresh lemonade, my favorite drink, through straws.

"Hmmm, RW, what does that mean?" PerryAnn ask.

"It means Road Way. I asked my dad the same thing when we saw a truck like that in town."

Three men in steel toed boots and hard hats stepped out of the truck, but Joe wasn't one of them. PerryAnn's eyes locked with one of the two younger men as they approached. "I've haven't seen him around here. I wonder if he lives in Albuquerque. How old do you think he is?" she whispered as she elbowed me in the ribs.

"Ouch, how should I know Pera?"

"Pera?"

"That's my new nickname for you. How do you like it?"

"It's good." She smiled and whispered, "That's Dirk. He's Grandma's nephew, so I guess he's related to me, but I don't understand how. It's some removed distant relative thing. They say he drinks and fights a lot."

Grandma Waters furrowed her brow at the site of Dirk. "What you doing here?"

"Well hello to you too, Grandma. We're here to stake a well location. Joe will come by later, when they get closer to drilling, to discuss a payment for damages to your farm." Grandma Waters face turned the color of blood.

"But he said no well would be near here," Grandma said. "He was here three weeks ago. Now you're here to put a well out there? How could he not know about well?"

"The company knows everything, and the men who buy the minerals rights only learn what they're told. They can change their mind after the land is bought, so Joe probably told you what he knew when he came here to buy. Anyway, Joe's green. He's only been buying for a few months. You have to look out for yourself," Dirk told her. "Why didn't you ask someone before you signed?"

"It was so much money he was talking about. He said just a small chance there would be well here. Is there anything I can do?"

"Not now. We have to get started." Dirk turned and walked toward the truck where the other two men were unloading their surveying equipment 500 feet from her house.

Now when Grandma Waters looked out her window, she would see a well in front of the pretty mountain view. She drilled into his back with her eyes. "What're you doing working for that company?"

When Dirk turned his head to the side as he walked away, you could see the scar over his right eye and his crooked nose. "Like you just said Grandma, money."

All the three men did that first morning was survey a one acre tract out of Grandma Waters forty acres and mark it with stakes. That evening, Grandma Waters came to my father to ask what she could do. He placed his hand on her shoulder and told her, "Nothing now. You signed the papers and took the money."

"I didn't know they could put a well on my farm," she said as she placed her hands on her head.

# CHAPTER FOUR

Two weeks after the men showed up to stake Grandma Waters' farm, Pera and I were sitting on the school steps waiting for middle school orientation. "Why are you going to seventh grade when you're fourteen?" I asked.

"I started late. My parents home schooled me." She looked down.

"Why'd they home school you? I wish I could be home schooled."

"They were busy with *Natives for Nature* and wanted me home. They got so busy, I had to take the year over. I really should be going to eighth, I guess."

"Do you mind being older than the other kids in your class?" I asked.

"No, I don't care," Pera replied.

There was a pause and I blurted, "Do you remember your birth?"

"No, do you?" She looked puzzled.

"Yah, I guess," I said.

"Why?" she asked.

"I had a dream last night where I was poking my head out and all these bright lights and strange eyes with white caps were peering down at me."

Pera laughed. "That's way too weird."

"I know, it was more like a memory than a dream," I said.

Pera changed the subject. "Grandma's drinking." She looked down at the ground as she spoke.

"She is?" I asked

"Yes, and she's mean when she drinks. Ever since Dad ran off the road she's been drinking two bottles of sangria wine every night," Pera said.

"Wow, I didn't know you could drink that much," I replied.

"My dad drank, but he wasn't drinking when they ran off the road."

"How do you know?" I asked.

She wrinkled her forehead and looked at me. "The tribal police chief called the house after he visited the farm that day. When I heard Grandma say his name, I picked up the phone in her room. He said there wasn't any alcohol in my father's blood, but he said there was a barricade on the road. My Dad had to swerve. He told Grandma there were extra marks on the road and asked her if she wanted to open an investigation. When she got off, I told her I wanted to see the photos of the tire marks and barricade."

"What'd she say?" I asked.

"She frowned at me and said she didn't want to investigate anything," Pera replied. Then Grandma said, "It isn't polite to speak of the dead."

"Oh, that's stupid," I said.

"I hate her right now. When I get the chance, I'm going to Albuquerque. I can live with the Moates," Pera said.

"Right, you want to find that boy who staked the farm." I was kidding, but not really. "Hey Pera, guess who I like." She didn't answer. "I like Bobby Martin, but he doesn't even know I am on the planet. When we ran into him at the bowling alley this summer, all he could do was stare at you."

"Yuck, he's not my type," she said. "I didn't know you liked him. I like the boy in the steel toed boots and the hard hat."

"Duh, I know since we've had the same conversation about him at least a hundred times since you saw him... I'm about to pull my hair out. Why don't you just ask how old he is?"

"I did," she said. "He's almost eighteen, but they don't want anyone to know because he's supposed to be eighteen to do that job. Dirk won't tell me his name, but he comes over from Albuquerque for the work."

"You're too young for him, you're not even fifteen yet," I said. "Gosh, I sound like my mother."

"No, I'm not! What do you mean?" she asked.

"I mean when I whispered to her that I wanted a bra last month, she practically yelled, "Matilda Louise you don't need a bra, you're too young. I'm sure everyone in the general store heard her because they all burst out laughing. I turned the color of cherry syrup. It felt like I was going to die. I was so embarrassed." As we sat on the school steps, I explained to Pera how furious I was at my mother.

She looked at me and said, "At least your mother is still alive."

The door to the school opened and we headed to the auditorium. A group of girls stared at us as we walked by to find our seats. They were girls from town, but when these girls, Neta and Jilly in particular, stared at Pera, she glared back fiercely. They sat in the row behind us, kicked her chair and chanted softly, *half-breed*, so she could hear. She wheeled around in her seat. "If you don't stop, I'm gonna get the principal."

"Wow, that was cool. When we get out of here, I want to tell you what happened to me with those girls," I whispered.

"Yeah, they stopped, but I bet they'll do it again," she replied.

On the way home, I told Pera about how those same girls had bullied me three months before her parents dropped her at the cactus farm. "They invited me to a slumber party at Neta's house. They'd been bullying me ever since it was announced that I had achieved the highest IQ scores, but I had thought they were through because they invited me to the party. I was excited to go.

Boy was I wrong. There were seven girls besides me. Neta's mother brought homemade chocolate chip cookies and milk into her room around eleven. Everything seemed ok until she came back in at one o'clock and said we had to go to bed. While we unfolded our sleeping bags, the others were whispering and laughing, but no one was talking to me.

Neta's mother came in and turned out the lights just as I got into my bag. When she closed the door, both Neta and Jilly unzipped their bags and jumped up."

"Is Neta the taller one with blonde, stringy hair?"

"Yeah, she's the gang leader," I replied.

"What happened next?" Pera asked.

"It was dark, but the dim light from the streetlight lit the room. I could see them start to dance around me. It was scary. They pretended to pee on me. Two of the others followed, and there were four of them dancing around my sleeping bag pretending to pee. They were chanting 'baby' and 'egghead,' but they were doing it softly, so no one could hear.

Their staring eyes bore down like they were at a tribal fire preparing to go to war. I got that they chanted egghead because of my IQ scores, but I couldn't figure out baby, except I'm the youngest in our grade. I just lay there while they danced around me pretending to pee and chanting.

When I tried to get out of my bag, one of the three girls sitting on the side took a pillow and put it over my head. It all went dark, and I could no longer see them peeing and dancing. I was trapped in my bag with a pillow over my head."

"Oh my gosh, MatiLou. What'd you do?"

"I yelled from under the pillow. Stop, I can't breathe. I can't breathe. I was crying and coughing and swinging my arms. They stopped, but I hit the closest ones to me, Neta and Jilly. My arm punched something hard. It was Neta's cheek. She was rubbing it with her hand when her mother burst into the room."

"What is going on in here?" she asked.

"The entire gang, all seven of them, told Neta's mother that I woke up out of a dream yelling and crying and swinging my arms. She believed them, and when I got home the next morning my mother believed them too."

"Matilda Louise, don't make up stories." She made me call Neta's mother to apologize for waking everyone up and hitting Neta on the cheek.

"Dad, you believe me, I pleaded," but he didn't stand up to her. They knew I'd had nightmares in the past and didn't believe the true story."

"Boy, MatiLou, that must have been horrible. I believe you," Pera said.

"You're the best," I replied. It felt like Pera was an angel, Indian princess, or maybe even my own lost sister, there to protect and watch over me.

"I've decided to go to the top of the hill in the park tomorrow. I wanna see if I can see Albuquerque," Pera changed the subject. After she'd locked eyes with the boy in the steel toed boots the day he came to stake Grandma Waters' farm, she'd started talking about moving to Albuquerque.

"Can I go?"

"I don't know. It is gonna be a hard trip over, but, yeah, I guess."

# CHAPTER FIVE

Rain wasn't mentioned on the news my mother watched as I marched by with my gear the next morning.

"Matilda Louise, don't be late for dinner again!"

"Okay." The door slammed behind me.

"How many times do I have to tell you not to slam the door?" my mother yelled.

"Sorry." I didn't tell her where I was going. She didn't ask.

At eight-thirty, I was outside Grandma Waters' house on my bike and called through the open bedroom window. "Let's go, Pera." String, a knife, my notes on how to make a trap, carrots, and a lunch pail with drinks and cookies were in the basket perched on the back fender. A lone black crow circled in the sky.

It was around nine o'clock when she finally emerged. "We're riding to the hill farthest from the farms, right?" I asked.

"Yup, that's what we said. That's the best view. We'll ride through the park to the trailhead and then hike to the top." I learned she'd hatched the plan after Dirk told her she could see Albuquerque from that hill.

"You're still gonna help me with the trap?" I asked.

"Yeah," Pera answered.

"Why are you gonna catch a rabbit?" she asked.

"I told you. I'm gonna trap. My father won't let me trap at the farm. I've been trying to catch one all summer. Anyway, rabbits around the farm are cottontails," I added. "I want a jackrabbit. I think there might be some on that hill."

As we rode at an easy pace past the end of Grandma Waters' fence and then ours, we could see the school in the distance. "Pera, what are you gonna do? I mean when you finish school?"

"I don't know. I guess something with *Natives for Nature*. Mr. Moate still runs it in Albuquerque."

"Sure," I rolled my eyes. *It's probably something to do with that boy in the steel toed boots.*

She glanced over at me. "You're rolling your eyes?" she asked.

"I am not."

"Whatever...Mr. Moate's wife kind of reminds me of Mom," she said. "It's her eyes. I wanna go see them in Albuquerque, but Grandma won't give me money for the bus."

"How much is it?" I asked.

"Twenty dollars. I still have ten dollars from my parents. I'll have to figure out how to get the rest. I've tried the number my dad used to call the Moates, but there's never an answer."

"Hmmm," I said.

"What're you gonna do when you finish school?" she asked.

"Me? I'm going to college. I'm gonna be a wildlife biologist."

"That's cool." She paused. "Hey, listen to this. Last night I dreamed I came into my room and crawled in bed. When I poked my head underneath to look for Spanky, strange looking boots were sitting there. Not steel toed, but old dirty ones, kind of like cowboy boots. I looked again, but they were gone. Then I woke up."

"That's really weird. Maybe it was a premonition?" I said.

"That's a big word," Pera replied.

"Yep, it means foreshadowing."

We crossed the road and were almost halfway to the school when Pera stopped and looked behind us to the farms. I slowed down and turned to see where she was looking and there, in the distance, was a small orange dot following us on the opposite side of the road. "Oh no, Spanky, watch out!" she yelled as she wheeled her bike around and peddled fast. A car was heading down the lane from the cemetery toward the spot where Spanky sat. *Was he deciding where to cross the road?* Pera stood up on her pedals and rode hard, but I couldn't keep up, so I pulled to the side about halfway from where he was sitting. While Pera headed toward Spanky on her bike, the car barreled toward them and suddenly stopped. The tires screeched as the driver pulled off the road. No other cars were coming or going. It was just that car, Pera and I on our bikes, and Spanky on the side of road.

When she reached Spanky, she scooped his furry body up, held him above her head with her arms outstretched and yelled at the top of her lungs, "You are a baaadddd cat!" She shouted back to me, "I'm taking him back. I don't know how he got out. My door was closed."

"Okay, I'll wait here."

The car slowly pulled back on the road, and as it passed me I saw the driver was an older man with a younger looking lady seated beside him. He screamed out the open window, "You girls better watch out." He drove forward, stopped, and the woman poked her head out. "He slammed the brakes so hard I got a whiplash and hit my knee on the dashboard!"

I'd never seen them or the car before. Maybe they were just passing through. "Yes ma'am, sorry. It was the cat." As he drove off, the black plume of smoke spitting out his tail pipe faded until it was a dot in the distance.

By the time Pera returned, I was about to pull my hair out. My watch was in my pocket, but I hadn't looked at it. My father had given it to me for my tenth birthday. "Be careful with it," he'd said. I figured Pera had been gone forty minutes because, for my experiments, I keep track of time by counting. I'd been sitting by the road practicing counting and getting restless when she had finally pulled beside me on her bike. I peeked at my watch. *Yep, forty minutes. Pretty good, MatiLou.* "What took so long?" I demanded.

"Grandma made me do the dishes I left in the sink," she said.

"Hurry, let's go, we barely have enough time to get up there and back. You didn't tell her where we're going, did you?"

"Nope," Pera said.

"How'd Spanky get out?" I asked.

"Through the cracked window. I forgot I cracked it to let a little air in when Grandma was cooking bacon. I hate the smell of bacon." She wrinkled her nose. "There was a tear in the screen and he slipped through."

We got back on our bikes and headed in the same direction we were going before Spanky's rescue. "We have to hurry now." We were both breathing pretty hard as we pushed the pedals of our bikes toward the school.

"Hey, I figure if we can make it down by six o'clock, we can ride home before dark. We're now an hour behind the schedule, but I still think there's time."

"You mean your schedule. Now I see why they called you egghead," she said.

"Shut up! I hate that word."

"Okay, chill out, I was just kidding."

We'd ridden about ten minutes when the corner to turn into the schoolyard or continue on to the park came into view. It was there, at the stop sign, we saw two girls standing next to their bikes. They were watching us riding down the road. From the distance, they looked like Neta and Jilly.

*Oh no, not again.*

"Isn't that tall girl Neta from the orientation?" Pera asked. She wore a ball cap and sunglasses like a disguise.

"Yup, that's Neta all right. She's the same one who kicked your chair and started the ambush on me at the slumber party. She is the meanest girl in school. Did I tell you it was her house I went to the night of the slumber party?"

"Yeah, you told me," Pera answered.

"The other one is Jilly. They were the two main ones who started dancing over me pretending to pee at the slumber party. Look, her hair looks so stupid, like a brillo pad. "

"We can handle them. Jilly is so short and dumpy! She can't be very strong. They're not much to be scared of, the two of them."

"Shhhh! Not so loud." No sooner had she said it than three more girls appeared from behind the garbage bin and walked toward Neta and Jilly. They weren't girls I knew and looked older, bigger and stronger, and boy did they look mean.

All the bikes were parked on the side of the road, and it looked like they were meeting with Neta and Jilly. There they were, all congregated at the stop sign we had to pass through on our way to the top of the hill. My heart felt like it had left my chest and lodged in my throat! "Should we turn around?"

"No," she snapped, not even slowing down. "If we do that, they'll never stop. Take a deep breath, sit up tall, look straight ahead and ride through."

"Are you sure?" I asked. "Those other girls look big, like guards on the football team. I haven't seen them before."

"Yeah, I know. They're big. Don't look. Just ignore them. Keep your head forward," Pera said.

I peddled so fast it felt like my legs were detached from my hips. "Slow down."

"Hurry," Pera called back to me. *I bet they heard that.* She was riding about twenty feet in front of me and slowed down so I could catch up. They stared at us as we rode by, but no one said a word.

When it seemed like we were in the clear, I turned to look back. They were still watching as Pera and I passed in front of the school. We turned left to the park and headed toward the entrance. "Whew, that was a close call," and just as I said it, Neta, Jilly and the biggest one of the other three girls came around the corner and chased us to the park fence. They were still at the stop sign when I'd looked back, but they must have taken a short cut through the school to the back gate. As they sprung out from behind the building, they chanted "egghead baby" and "half-breed" and tried to block us from passing. *Oh boy, we're outnumbered.*

I'd never seen anything like what I saw next. It happened so fast. Pera came to a screeching stop, got off her bike. She walked over to Neta and yelled, "Get off your bike." None of us, Jilly, me or the other girl, moved an inch. It was so quiet you could hear the leaves rustle in the trees.

A ray of sunlight peeked through the clouds and lit Pera up. She looked like an Indian princess as she towered over Neta with her arms on her hips. Neta acted like a startled mouse about to be eaten. It seemed like an hour, but it was probably a couple of minutes before, cowering on her bike, Neta just turned her wheels around and headed back down the road with Jilly and the other girl following.

"Wow," I looked at Pera in awe. "Why didn't I stand up to them at the slumber party the way you just did? I could've kicked at them, but instead I cried and lay perfectly still. I didn't know what to do."

"Yeah, but didn't you say there were seven of them, and they had a pillow over your head? They might have smothered you."

"Guess I'll never know," I said under my breath.

Pera got back on her bike. "Let's go."

My heart was throbbing in my throat, but now it slowly pounded in my chest. I pushed my weight down to move the pedals forward, stretched my arms out, and straightened my legs. "I'll stand up to those thugs if I ever get cornered again," I vowed. "Look, a crow," I said. "I wonder if it's the one that circled when I waited for you this morning, Pera." *Is he following us?* There was a knot in my stomach as we rode.

We peddled faster and faster as we drew closer to the park entrance. "Look, there it is. There's the top," she yelled. "We'll be able to see Albuquerque."

"Yeah, we'll see it if it's clear," I said looking up at the mountain of clouds building in the sky. "Slow down. I can barely keep up."

She dropped her pace and rode beside me as we approached the gate. No one manned the guardhouse. A note on the chalkboard by the door, which read 'Back in 10 Minutes,' caught my eye. Beside it was a slot for money and a sign – '$1 for pedestrians; $5 for cars with two; $7 for cars with three or more,' but nothing written about bikes. We rode through without dropping any money in the slot. "I wonder if we should leave an IOU. Do you have a pen?" I asked.

"No," she said.

As we pulled away from the gatehouse, we grabbed two park maps.

"Here's the road that leads to the hill," Pera pointed to a spot on the map. "It looks like the trail starts by the parking lot."

"Ok, but let's hurry," I turned to look at where she pointed, and it loomed before us more like a mountain than a hill. We'd lost time on Spanky shortly followed by Neta's ambush. I pulled my watch from my pocket. "It's eleven-thirty now. I thought we'd be at the top by noon," I said.

"Look, it's not that far from here." Pera pointed toward the hill. We rode another thirty minutes before we reached the parking lot. "Let's hide our bikes behind these bushes," she said. There were no cars in the lot, but we still hid them from view. We took our stuff off the bikes. I looked in my lunch pail, which housed oatmeal cookies and drinks. My mouth watered so much I thought I might drool.

"Boy, I'm hungry. Do you wanna eat these cookies?" I asked.

"No, come on. We can eat at the top," she answered.

"Do you have anything for lunch in your pack?"

She grinned. "I made a couple of cheese sandwiches when I washed the dishes for Grandma. I have a canteen with water, too."

"Yeah, and I have nuts and jellybeans from the general store, too," I said.

We put all the food and drinks in her pack and agreed to take turns carrying it up the hill. On the map, a trail to the top veered right.

As we started on our way, the beginning of the path was easy; the views on both sides displayed desert and hills. It was beautiful. We saw chipmunks poke their heads out of the ground, a couple of mule deer grazing, lots of squirrels jumping through small brush trees and a few jackrabbits scampering around. "Ha, just as I suspected," I muttered to myself. "Plenty of jackrabbits here."

"What?" Pera called over her shoulder.

"Nothing."

"You need to keep up. You're going too slow," she yelled. She was in front. Her legs seemed at least twice as long as mine. She was carrying the pack and still had to stop and wait for me to catch up. Looking back at how far we'd come and then ahead, I guessed it would take another hour before we even reached the base of the hill. It didn't look nearly that far on the map.

I pulled my watch from my pocket, but this time put it on my wrist. The face was big enough to house a compass, and it looked huge on my skinny arm. "You'll grow into it," my father said when he gave it to me. "We have to start back by four o'clock to get home by dark," I said.

"If you'd hurry up we could make it. You're driving me crazy. You're acting like a policeman about the time," Pera snapped.

"Tough, maybe I'm acting like that or maybe I'm just trying to make sure we get home before dark!"

"Calm down. We'll get back," she said.

*Right, all you can think about is getting to the hilltop so you can see how far it is to Albuquerque and the boy with the steel toed boots.* "Hey, the nuts! Do you want to eat them now? I'm starving." She ignored me and kept going. I wanted to get my hands on the nuts in her pack. It was taking longer than I thought it would to get to the top. We didn't even start the climb from the base until two o'clock.

"It's not too steep here," she said.

"Yeah, but it's a rocky path. It's not even a little smooth or cleared." *The rocks are piercing my feet through my shoes.*

About halfway up, the trail split into two. "Look, here are two trails," Pera said. We chose the direct path with a sign that pointed straight up to the top.

"Pera, do you want me to carry the pack?" I asked. Boy did I want to get my hands on the nuts.

"I said no, you're slowing us down already. Just try to keep up. Get a stick. It'll help you climb," she answered. We looked around and it was several minutes before we each found one sturdy enough to use. The clouds in the sky, no longer white and puffy, were now dark and joined together.

"Rain. I saw the forecast this morning and there wasn't any rain, but that looks like a storm," I said.

"Maybe," she looked up.

"My tennis shoes aren't too good for this," I said as I double knotted my shoelaces. "The soles are slick and they're thin. The rocks are jabbing my feet. And I'm getting tired."

"Stop complaining, we're almost there," Pera said.

"Yeah, well your shoes look like they have tread," I said.

"You're not the only one with problems. My ankles hurt. I should have worn my other high top shoes," she snapped.

*I wish I hadn't come.*

It got rocky and steep fast. At about three quarters of the way to the top, I looked at my watch again.

"Pera, it's now three-thirty. We have to turn around!"

She acted like she didn't hear me and just kept moving up the trail with her back to me. *I'm so annoyed. She won't listen to me.*

"PerryAnn, we have to turn back!" I screamed.

"Come on. We're almost there. I promise we'll turn back when we get to the top." She didn't even turn around as she said it, but kept climbing.

I looked up. Closer to the top, the rocky path went straight up until it smoothed out to gradual switchbacks.

Trees lined it, offering some protection from falling off the trail at the edge. They also hid the view of our climb. No one knew we were in the park. No one could see our ascent. No one would find our bikes hidden in the brush.

*If only my mother knew where I was.* We were almost to where the path smoothed out to the switchback when I put the stick into the ground to take my next step over a small boulder in the way. It snapped; I lost my balance and fell backward.

"You okay, MatiLou?" Pera yelled.

"Yeah, I managed to not hit my head, but I think my ankle's twisted." I got up and took a step. "Yep," I cried. "Ouch, I think it's twisted."

"It'll feel better if you keep going," she said. "Come on, you can make it."

My ankle was hurting, and it seemed like forever limping back and forth, one direction and then the other to the top. Pera was sitting on a boulder above me, watching, as

I made my final ascent. It was four o'clock when I reached her. *Oh great, we're at the top and now we have to start down.* "What time does the sun set?" I asked.

"I think it was eight-thirty last night, but we still have light after that," Pera said.

"Yeah, but it took us till now to get up here from the parking lot. That was before I hurt my ankle. We'll never get back by dark, and it's going to rain any second. My mother's gonna kill me!" It was the first time I'd really wanted to hit Pera in the whole time I'd known her that summer. She'd made us late with that stupid cat of hers, and she'd pushed me to come up here when I knew we didn't have enough time. I felt knots in my stomach like the ones I'd get when my mother would yell out the back door "Matilda Louise!"

"Come, you have to see!" Pera was standing ten feet above me on a rock. My ankle felt tender as I limped to where she sat. She reached out to help me up. *Wow, the view!* To the east you could see the horizon, and to the west the skyline of Albuquerque. There was a road adjoining the empty parking lot below, which looked like it led directly there, and the way down was an easy path. It didn't appear long, like the steep, rocky four mile trail we'd just climbed. The sun, now lower in the sky, was hidden from view behind the hills and cast an orange hue on the desert.

"Boy, it looks a lot easier to get up here from this side," I said.

"Yeah, but it would have been way too far on our bikes. We'd have had to find a ride," Pera answered.

*Yeah, and maybe if we'd done that someone would know we're here.* "If we're gonna try to get home before dark, we have to go now! I'm not even gonna have time to build a trap for the jackrabbits. We wouldn't make it down in time."

"Yes, we can," Pera snapped. "There's plenty of time. Go ahead and work on your stupid trap. Like I said, we still have light after sunset for about forty-five minutes. Going down will be much faster. Do you want me to help?"

*I'll do it myself.* "No." I picked up the pack and stepped off the rock with my good ankle. After searching for a few minutes, I decided to set the trap not far from where we'd been standing. Working fast, I pulled my rope and directions from the pack and set the food out. The idea wasn't to injure the rabbit, just to catch it. *I'll get my dad to come back with me to check it. We can drive to the other side and take the shorter trail to the top. Maybe he won't be as mad when he sees my catch.*

Just when I'd finished building my trap with straw, sticks and leaves, it started to pour rain. I hurried back to where Pera stood with the pack in my hand, and we huddled under a rock where the overhang provided a space to sit comfortably. The rain drove hard. Leaves from surrounding trees protected us from the pelting downpour. It was like we were under siege from thousands of arrows for an hour; there was nothing to do but wait it out. We stayed pretty dry and safe from the sting of the drops, but the rain was so heavy, we couldn't see the tree where I set my trap twenty feet away. We sat in silence. I sighed real loud and closed my eyes. I was mad at Pera for making us late, mad at her for pushing us to the top and mad she wouldn't turn around. The sky cleared and it was seven-thirty. "Now what, Pera?"

"It's too late to start down now. It'll be wet and slick. With your ankle hurt, we can't get back to the parking lot before dark," she said.

*It's official. No one knows we were on the road earlier except the man and lady in the car that almost hit Spanky. No one knows we rode by the school except Neta and her gang. Not even the park rangers know we're here. Not even my mother.*

"Great. If it wasn't for Spanky, it would be six-thirty, and we would still have time!" I yelled.

"Right and if it wasn't for your ankle, we could try it now. Anyway, you could have turned back," she yelled at the top of her lungs. I was startled. We sat in silence another thirty minutes. "Look, the moon is out. It's full. The sky is clear," she said.

"It's a good thing since we don't have a light up here," I sneered.

"Please don't be mad. I'm sorry," Pera said. "I thought we could get back. We have our sandwiches, the food and drinks you brought, and we can sleep under this ledge. Come on, it'll be fun, like camping. In the morning, we can go to the parking lot and wait for someone to give us a ride back to our bikes."

Pera unloaded the food and drinks we'd brought from the pack. "I'm starving. I haven't eaten since I left my house this morning," I said as she handed me a sandwich. My mouth was watering.

"I ate some peanut butter and crackers when I made theses cheese sandwiches," Pera said.

*What? She could have brought me some.* I devoured my sandwich, popped open a grape soda and handed it to Pera.

"You drink it," she said. "I have my canteen. Just drink one though, and save the other two for tomorrow." When we finished the sandwiches and cookies, I started to open the nuts and the jellybeans, but she stopped me. "Save that for tomorrow."

The sun sank on the horizon. It was twilight, but the moon had already risen and provided plenty of light to see. My notebook, trap instructions, the New Mexico wildlife list, string and my knife were by my side. Pera's canteen and a piece of paper with an address written in red ink lay beside the open pack. She started to thumb through my notebook.

"What are you doing?" I asked. A poem I'd written in the spring for an English assignment fell out.

"Hey, is this your poem?" Pera questioned.

"Yes, give it to me." I said. "I snatched at the paper, but grabbed only air."

She jumped up, out of my reach and started to read.

One Match

She cries, "Lucky, come boy come."
No stir from the forest is heard.
A tear streams down her cheek,
her legs tremble, a stir, a bird.

Cinders crackle, smolder.
A sparrow lights on her shoulder.
Where can Lucky be?

Last night a bright glow, as big as the sun,
lit the whole sky and ground too.
The glow was so high,
the sky and the earth were one.

Screams were heard as hides were scorched.
Eggs cracked, trees crashed.
Young ran with old, flames licked at heels.

One torch, one match, one flick of a hand,
one careless thought turned deed.
Or was it intent? Was it greed?

The girl looks down, at the ground,
scorched and charred and black.
Oh Lucky, my friend, my dog, my hound,

did you have to go see?
And out of the thicket, a whimper, a cry.

"Hey that's pretty cool. You could be a poet," she smiled.

"Nope, I told you I'm going to be a biologist. I got an A though. Give it back."

She handed it to me. "Why'd you write about a fire?" she asked.

"Because they had one in the national forest around Los Alamos. I didn't know how it started and it upset me when I saw smoke plumes and flames light the sky. I wondered if the animals got out. The teacher forced me to read my poem in front of the whole class. When I finished she told everyone that I'd be moving to a room for gifted children next year because I'd made the highest marks on the IQ test."

"Wow, that's embarrassing. Why'd she do that?"

"Who knows? But after that the girls in class stopped talking to me, and started whispering so I couldn't hear." I paused. "My father won't let me have a dog. He'd trained a Husky when he was in Antarctica and brought him home. He hasn't had another dog since.

"Why won't he let you have a dog?" she asked.

"He says the wild animals are my pets, and it would bark and scare them away. If I had a dog, he'd be a hound, and I'd name him Lucky."

We heard a scream. "Pera, is that a woman?" I shuddered.

"It's an animal. Listen," she said. It screamed again. It was pretty far away, but closer than the first time. I looked at the wildlife list.

"Could it be an owl?" I pondered out loud.

"No, but it sounds like coyotes are on the attack." There was barking and then the scream again.

It was a horrendous scream. I read the animal list out loud, "Coyotes, black bears, jaguars, javelinas, cougars, bobcat and wolves…"

"Crap, I think it was a javelina," she said.

*That's the first time she's cussed.* "Black bears are listed too," I said.

"I know they're around, but I hadn't thought of that. We need to put that food up in the tree. I hope there's enough light to see since we don't have a flashlight," she said.

*Right, because we weren't planning to be up here after dark! My parents are gonna be so mad! I'd better take the trap down in the morning. I'm in enough trouble without disobeying Dad about the trap.* "We're lucky the moon is full," I muttered.

"What?" Pera asked.

"Nothing, I was just talking to myself." We decided to hoist the pack with the food in it into the tree furthest from the rock where we planned to sleep. It was farther than the tree where I set the trap and was about thirty feet away. We used my string to lift the pack to the lowest branch, about ten feet high, and returned to the rock for the night. Pera's canteen, my knife, the maps and all the papers were in a pile by my side.

I looked around on the ground. "Hey, there was a piece of paper laying here. Did you pick it up?"

"Yup," she said.

"What was on it?" I asked.

"It's the Moate's phone number. It must have been in my pack from the last time I tried to call them."

*Weird. I thought it was an address.* I looked at my watch. Between eating, all our talking, and stringing Pera's pack in the tree, three hours had passed. *It will be morning before we know it.*

As we huddled under our ledge, we still heard hooting and barking in the distance. "I guess this is pretty fun. I'm glad we have light from the moon, but all the animal screams are scary," I said.

"Yeah, it doesn't look like anyone has camped here, so no killers will find us," Pera replied.

"Oh, I hadn't thought of that. You're scaring me." I said.

"Don't be scared, we'll be fine." She laughed.

"It's not funny! Anyway my parents are probably gonna kill me tomorrow." *I wonder what they are doing. They're probably looking for me right now.*

I paused for a few minutes. "Boy, you sure let Neta have it today."

"What'd she do?" Pera asked.

"When you looked down at her, she shrunk about six inches. Neta's a complete whimp. I can't believe I let her terrorize me at the slumber party. Jilly is just a spineless worm, too. They're both creeps."

Pera laughed again. *Why is that funny?* Boy I'm glad that happened today. You didn't let them bully us."

"I guess," Pera said.

"Yeah and I wonder why all the girls at the stop sign didn't come after us with Neta and Jilly?"

"I don't know, but be glad. That would have been five against two," Pera replied.

"Yeah, I know. Neta isn't as big of a gang leader as she thinks. Next time I see her, I'm gonna call her 'baby.'"

"Remember, at the slumber party there were seven against you, MatiLou. I wouldn't do that. Just let it go. Neta's a bully.

"Hmmm, maybe."

"I mean it. You don't want to get her mad. Just leave her alone. Ignore her." I thought about what she said as I looked up. In the moonlight, white wisps streaked across the sky. Thoughts were flooding my mind. "I wonder what it was like to live like the Indians out in the open, day and night, breathing fresh air, only taking from the earth what they needed to survive."

"Yeah, well if you're gonna live like an Indian, you better toughen up your feet," Pera said.

"What do you mean?" I asked.

"You couldn't even make it up this hill with tennis shoes on today without whining," she said.

"Ha ha, very funny." *She's getting on my nerves.* "Listen! What I mean is they respected the land, nature, and the creatures. I like their ways. Maybe it's because of my mother's ancestors."

"Don't be so corny." Pera said.

"I'm not being corny!" I snapped. "What I mean is the drillers and people like that take more than their share from the earth."

"Is that your high IQ talking again?" she sneered.

"Shut up about my IQ. I wish I'd never told you about that."

"Really, you sound like a nerd," Pera said. "Chill out."

*That's it. I'm not telling her anything else. She's being mean. I'm not saying another word to her.* My mind began to wander again. *I wonder, if I had a tribal name what it would be?*

We sat in silence for what seemed like hours. The animal screams came closer and closer. It was starting to freak me out.

*I'll write a poem to pass the time. I wish I had a pen.*

*Respect nature,*
*Take what you need,*
*But do it nicely,*
*Like Indians were....*

I said it over and over in my head until finally I couldn't stand it any longer. "Pera, are you asleep?" I whispered.

"No."

"Are you thinking about the boy with the steel toed boots?" I was joking, but not really. She'd mentioned him again today on the way up the hill.

Pera sighed. "No, I was thinking about my mother's parents. They're trying to get me to come live with them. They think I'll be better off than I am with Grandma."

"In Oklahoma? That's terrible."

"I know. I don't want to go. I heard Grandma on the phone with them again. She told them I wanted to live with her, but she was slurring her words. That didn't help." She paused. "I hope she remembers to feed Spanky."

I didn't know what to say to Pera. She'd been through her parent's accident and now this. I knew her grandma drank because I smelled it on her breath. "I don't want you to go either," was all I could think to say. I lay awake and thought how terrible it would be if she left. "Pera," I whispered. She was now lying with her eyes closed. "I need to pee."

"Just go over there a few feet."

I didn't want to go, especially since she'd mentioned killers, but it was that or pee on our nice dry spot under the ledge.

I stepped just a few feet away. *That's much better.* "Why don't you want to go to college?" I asked crawling back under the ledge. "You could work for *Natives for Nature* after you finish. You could be a lawyer like Mr. Moate or you could study something else that would help."

"Darn it, MatiLou, too many questions. I never said I didn't wanna go to college. I said I'd probably work for *Natives for Nature* like my dad."

"Okay ... one more question. Has anyone come back again? I mean about the stakes on the farm? I wonder if they're going to put a well on your farm."

She rolled over and yawned. "No one has contacted Grandma or come back as far as I know. It'll be awful if they put a well out there in her front yard."

"How far do you figure it would be from her cactus garden? It shouldn't bother them, the cactus, should it?"

"The cactus?" She sat up. "No, it isn't that. People could still drive up to buy them. Dirk told us the pits from the well shouldn't pollute.

"If they won't pollute the cactus, then what else bothers you?" I asked.

"It's the noise and the ugliness. It's what my dad fought," Pera replied.

"I couldn't believe your grandma sold her mineral rights that day. I was right there when she did it, too," I said.

"I know. Why didn't you come get me?" Pera asked.

"Remember, you'd yelled at me to get out of your room," I replied.

"I did? Dad would roll over in his grave if he knew," Pera said.

"Maybe he does," I answered. "There's a grave at the cemetery that says,

> 'Where I once was, so you are now.
> Where I am now, you soon shall be.
> So come my friend and follow me.'"

"Creepy," Pera said. "Which one?"

"I don't know, just one of the graves. Did you hear that?" I grabbed her arm.

"What?" She yawned again.

"There it is. Breathing. Something's out there. I hear breathing." I jerked my head around and strained to listen. It was in the direction of the tree where we'd put the pack. "There it is again." I inched closer to her. "Did you hear it?" We poked our heads up and peeked over the ledge we were under. The brush was moving in the breeze, and in the moonlight we saw a small black bear grunting and breathing heavily as he attempted to pull her pack from the tree. It was within reach of his paw, but he couldn't snap the string. We'd tied it well. We stayed frozen in our spots for almost an hour while he pawed at the pack before finally moving into the brush.

"Whew," Pera said. "That was scary."

"No kidding I hope he doesn't have a mama lurking out there in the bushes," I said.

"He was small, but I don't think it was a baby," Pera replied.

"I hope not. He wasn't that small. Did you hear that? There it is, rustling again. I hope he's not coming back." I whispered. For thirty minutes, we sat with our eyes glued onto the spot where the bear had entered the brush, but he didn't return.

"I think he's gone," Pera said and turned over onto her side.

I pulled out the notebook to look for the wildlife list, and a second poem I'd written fell out, only this time she didn't see it. I read over it quickly before slipping it back in between the pages.

*A Conversation with the River*

"Where are you going?"
"I am going to the sea."
"Oh please take me."

"Oh please take me."
"Please take me with you to the sea."
"Jump in and come along."
"But I don't have a boat that's strong."

"You don't need a boat."
"Jump in and on my surface float."

"Stretch your arms out wide."
"And on my current you can glide."

"But what if I sink or hit a rock?"
"I feel dead weight like a block."
"Breathe in and out to adjust the weight."
"Let your breath help you navigate."

"Okay, I am scared, but here I go."
"I am breathing now and going slow."
"It's cold and wet, but I feel free."
"What will we do when we reach the sea?"
"Enjoy the ride, breathe and just be."

It sounded like I'd written it about Grandma Waters, but it couldn't be, because I wrote it before I knew how Grandma Waters got her name.

"What are you doing? What time is it?" Pera asked as she rolled onto her back.

I looked at my watch. "It's three o'clock." *The sun will rise in a few hours.* "Maybe we should sleep."

"Hooray," she said. "Okay, we'll take turns. You go first."

My ankle throbbed as I lay my head on a soft mat of straw and leaves and took a deep breath of crisp night air.

"Ahhh…" I closed my eyes and drifted into sleep. The coyotes still barked in the distance, but I managed to weave them into my dream where I was an Indian princess. We were moving our camp for the winter and everywhere around were teepees filled with members of our tribe. In my teepee with me was Bobby Martin. *Bobby Martin was my warrior?* He was the fair-haired boy who didn't even know I was on the planet. The hound dog, Lucky, from my poem was in there, too. A fire burned, sparks flew, and lots of animal skin rugs were on the teepee walls and around us on the ground. On one rug was the head of the small black bear that had tried to steal our pack from the tree. Bobby and I were about to kiss when horses tethered outside began to neigh and stamp their feet.

A loud thud awakened me out of my dream, and I opened my eyes to see the dawn of morning had arrived. The rising sun hadn't yet peeked over the horizon, but the owls had ceased hooting and the coyotes were no longer barking.

It was silent as I looked around to see Pera wasn't there with me under our ledge. *Maybe she stepped away to pee or to view Albuquerque in the distance again, or cut the pack from the tree.*

There was a chill in my bones. I felt stiff like a lizard when it gets cold, but my ankle wasn't throbbing. *Good, not much swelling.* In the night, I'd rested my foot on a rock a little higher than the ground. I rotated it left and right. *Seems ok.* I stretched my legs and arms and sat up. Boy was I thirsty. I looked around for Pera's canteen, but it was nowhere in sight.

I got up and stepped on top of the ledge to look for her, but she wasn't by the trees, the one my trap was under, or the one where we hung the pack. "Pera," I called, but she didn't respond. "Hello," I yelled. Hello, hello, hello echoed back. "Pera," I screamed.

The silence was spooky like the animal screams we'd heard in the night. I lifted myself onto the rock where we'd stood and looked at the parking lot below. There were no cars in the lot, and no sign of Pera.

When I returned to where we'd slept, I saw the pack. I hadn't seen it before, but there it was on top of the ledge, cut from the tree. Next to the pack were my notes, string, and my two remaining drinks. My knife was gone. On top of my papers was a note from her. *Where'd she find a pen?* The note said, "MatiLou. I'm sorry, but I had to go. I took half the nuts and jellybeans. Just follow the map. You know the way down. You'll be fine." She'd left one of the two trail maps we'd picked up at the guard gate.

I walked to the other side again and peered down at the parking lot and the road that led to Albuquerque. *Still no cars in the lot.* "Pera," I screamed, but again no reply, only the echo of my scream. I sat on top of the rock as tears welled up in my eyes and my throat closed so I couldn't breathe. I cried. "PerryAnn," I screamed at the top of my lungs. Still there was nothing but the sound of my voice echoing off the rocks. I took one more look down the hill. Now there was a car traveling toward Albuquerque.

"Okay MatiLou, Pera left you up here! You're gonna have to get down by yourself," I said under my breath. My voice felt hoarse from screaming. *Why would she do that? She wouldn't. But her note says she would.* I read it again. "MatiLou. I'm sorry, but I had to go. I took half the nuts and jellybeans. Just follow the map. You know the way down. You'll be fine." There it was. She'd left me on the hill. I wiped the tears from my face.

"Okay, if you're there, and the preacher and a bunch of other people say you are, can you please help me get down off this mountain? And can you please watch over Pera? I don't know where she is. I hope you do. Amen." I heard the flap of wings, but there was nothing in the sky. I hoped it wasn't the black crow we'd seen.

I remembered what my mother had told me when we'd seen a crow circling overhead on our way one Saturday to the farmers' market. "The crow could be a symbol of wisdom, or it could be a foreboding of bad happenings, even a death," she'd said. When I got home that day, I looked up foreboding in Webster's. *Was the crow Pera and I had seen yesterday foreboding death? Maybe it was the animal we heard screaming when coyotes barked last night?* I looked up again and there it was – a lone black crow.

I picked up the pack, pulled out one of the two sodas and popped open the top. Instead of going down to the parking lot to wait for a ride, I decided to make my way back on the trail we'd ascended. My parents had pounded it into my head to never get into a car with a stranger. Anyway, the lot was empty, and I was ready to get started. As I gulped down the soda, I studied the trail map. My ankle was now a little stiffer than when I'd woken up. I tried to circle it. *Not as good as I thought.*

The sun hung low in the sky, but provided enough warmth, so I wouldn't be too cold on my way down the hill.

With Pera's stick in my hand and her pack on my back, I started my descent.

"Ah, this is easier than yesterday," I muttered. My watch said nine o'clock. Where had the two hours gone since I'd heard the thud and found Pera missing? I came to the rocky part of the trail, and there I sat. *A few nuts and jellybeans would be good.* I stuffed them in my mouth. "That's good together. Nuts and jellybeans. I'll do that again," I said to myself. I checked to see where I was on the map. *Yep, this is the trail.* Maybe I wasn't as tired as yesterday because it seemed easier to descend.

When I reached the bottom of the rocks, I started on my way through the desert floor. Bright colors of flowers in bloom reflected the morning sun, and I was so busy taking in their beauty that I wasn't watching where I was on the trail. "Ouch." I brushed against a prickly pear cactus and several needles lodged in my thigh. "Ouch. Dang it." I stopped and pull them out one by one. "Ouch, ouch, ouch." I counted twenty in my thigh. When I pulled the last one out I saw, out of the corner of my eye, the tail end of a snake vanishing into the brush. It'd crawled across the path not thirty feet in front of me. I decided it was a rattlesnake. It wasn't coiled, but was making way maybe to an unsuspecting meal or to soak up sun on a rock. *Wow, that was lucky...* the cactus stopped me from walking further on the trail and stepping on the snake.

The preacher had said at Pera's parent's funeral, "There are no mistakes in God's plan," but I didn't have a clue what he meant until now. *Did God hear my prayer? Was the cactus my answer?* I'd been enjoying the scenery, and the beauty of nature had saved me from a snake that could have killed me. *I still don't understand how Pera's parents' car accident or Pera leaving me out here could be God's plan. I guess I still don't understand what he meant.*

The morning sun on the desert stole my thoughts. *Being a wildlife biologist will be perfect for me. Out in nature with the creatures.* Like yesterday, I saw chipmunks poke their heads out of the ground, mule deer grazing, squirrels jumping through trees and jackrabbits scampering here and there. *Crap.* "I forgot to check the trap this morning for a jackrabbit," I said to myself. *I have to get back to check it.*

Thoughts of Pera crept into my mind even though I tried to keep them out. The truth is I was furious with her for leaving me there. I felt my face turn beet red when I thought about it. Where had Pera gone? How could she leave without my hearing her? Where was she now?

The next sign I came to read one mile to the trailhead. "I'm gonna make it." I blew the hair out of my face and proceeded. After another thirty minutes, I reached the parking lot where Pera and I had hidden our bikes. I looked at my watch. *Wow, only two hours. Pera was right. We could have made it down if it hadn't rained.* It'd taken half the time to reach the parking lot from the top, as it had to go up yesterday. I brought both bikes out from behind the brush.

Two hikers, a man and a woman retrieving their backpacks from their truck, spotted me. The blood and a tear on my pants where the cactus had stuck me, plus dirt on my shirt, my arms, and probably my face must have caught their eye. The man yelled, "Hey, do you need a hand?"

"Yeah, can you take me to the ranger gate?" I asked. He loaded the bikes into the bed of his truck and drove to the park entrance gate.

The ranger came out and helped the man unload the bikes. We walked inside and I told him what had happened to Pera and me since we'd passed through the unmanned guardhouse the day before. "We passed through the gate and hid our bikes in bushes at the parking lot," I explained to the ranger. He listened as I reported that no one was on the trail, so no one had seen us as we made our ascent up the hill.

A helicopter flew over so close we had to stop talking while it passed. "They are looking for you," the ranger said. He told me Grandma Waters and my parents had called the police last night at ten o'clock, and the police had called the park. They were waiting until today to start a search in case we turned up in the middle of the night. "This morning the police provided the park with this bulletin," he added as he pointed at the paper before us. It read, Missing PerryAnn Waters and MatiLou Butler with pictures under both names. "Where is the other girl?" he asked.

"I don't know," I answered and reached in the pack for Pera's note. He glanced at the note and picked up the phone to make a call. "I have one girl here," he said to the voice on the line. "No." He looked at the paper and then me. "MatiLou is the one here. The other girl, PerryAnn, is still missing." For thirty more minutes I told him about our hike up the trail, our night there, and what had happened when I'd found PerryAnn was missing. He loaded both bikes into his truck and drove me to the farm.

It was the longest drive I ever made. I didn't know what I'd find when I got home. Would my mother kill me or be glad to see me? Would she make me apologize? And to whom I did not know.

When we drove up the drive, my mother ran out of the house with my father following behind. As I got out of the truck, she hugged me tightly. I could barely breathe. The tears in her eyes dripped onto her shirt. "Thank God, MatiLou! Don't ever do that again," she scolded. My father stepped up and put his arms around us both.

"Is PerryAnn home?" I asked. My parents looked at each other and then at me and shook their heads no.

Grandma Water's was standing in her cactus garden when the ranger truck pulled into our drive. She yelled, "Is PerryAnn with you?" and started running across the field.

"No, I was hoping she was home with you," my father yelled back. When she reached where my mother and father, the ranger, and I stood, she looked tired, but I didn't smell alcohol on her breath. The ranger asked Grandma Waters a bunch of questions about Pera and her friends, and before he left said, "We'll continue to search with the helicopter. The radio station will make announcements, but the search with police cars won't begin until twenty-four hours after you reported her missing, so that will be at ten o'clock tonight."

After he drove away, Mother, Dad, and I stood in the front yard with Grandma Waters. She grilled me about what had happened since we'd left her farm the day before. I told her how we'd ridden past the school. "Pera stood up to Neta and her gang."

"Her name is PerryAnn. I don't like that name," she snapped.

"Okay," I said. I told her how PerryAnn had the idea to put the pack in the tree to keep the bears from taking our food. And I showed her the note she'd left for me to read.

# CHAPTER SIX

PerryAnn and the man who picked her up sat in silence for a few minutes as he drove down the road. He smelled strange. It wasn't a smell she knew. She looked down at his boots, "Are those the kind of boots you wear on a drilling rig?"

"What do you think?" he snapped. When she'd gotten into the car, he'd told her he'd been working on a rig the night before. He wasn't wearing steel toed boots like the men who came to stake the farm. Instead, he was wearing dirty cowboy boots kind of like the ones she'd seen under her bed in her dream. He stepped on the gas and continued toward Albuquerque and after thirty minutes of traveling in silence, he turned on a dirt road.

"Where are you going?" PerryAnn asked. "This isn't the way to Albuquerque." She felt the pulse racing in her neck. He took one hand and then the other off the wheel and rolled up his sleeves. Out of the corner of her eye, she looked at his arm. A tattoo of a lady with a fish tail and a knife through her chest covered his forearm. "Where are we going? she demanded.

He didn't answer her question, turned on the radio and continued down the road.

"Hey, what are you doing?" she screamed.

He looked straight ahead, "Shut up. I need to make a stop down this road." Patsy Cline was singing her heart out when the music stopped. "We have an alert that a young girl fourteen years old is missing." The announcer went on to describe PerryAnn. "Tall, long brown hair, brown eyes…"

The man looked carefully at her. "Shit," he said.

"If anyone has seen her, please call the police immediately," the announcer continued.

The man slammed on his breaks, put the car in reverse, punched his foot hard on the gas and pulled onto the highway. "Get out," he ordered. PerryAnn opened the door and barely closed it before he floored the gas pedal and sped away.

She was standing by the side of the road when a truck traveling in the distance reached her. A woman rolled down the window, "Do you need help?" She wasn't listening to the radio.

"Yes, can you take me to this address?" PerryAnn asked.

The woman looked at it. "Sure, I know exactly where that is, but you will have to ride in back." PerryAnn crouched in the corner behind bales of hay as a helicopter flew overhead. It hovered for a moment over the truck and then flew away. They traveled several miles down the road when PerryAnn saw that the car she'd been traveling in with the man was pulled to the side. A policeman was standing at his window. The man saw her crouched in the back of the truck and as they drove by, his staring eyes met hers. She glared at him and breathed a sigh of relief as they passed his car.

Thirty minutes later, the woman turned the pickup into Jim and Betty Moate's driveway. "Thanks for the ride," PerryAnn said as she jumped out of the truck.

She was walking to the front door when Betty opened it and yelled. "Jim, she's here."

Jim came to the door. "We heard they were looking for you on the radio. Thank God. What are you doing here?" He waved to the woman as she backed out of the drive. He then turned and stepped into the house, picked up the phone and called Grandma Waters.

"Let me speak to her," Grandma Waters asked him. He handed the phone to PerryAnn.

"No, Grandma. No, I didn't. I'm sorry. I love you, too." PerryAnn handed the phone to Mr. Moate.

While she devoured the pancakes Betty had prepared, PerryAnn explained why she'd come to Albuquerque. "Mr. Moate, I tried to call you, but no one ever answered. My mother's parents are trying to take me from Grandma Waters.

They want me to live with them in Oklahoma. They notified child protective services to investigate. I saw a letter they sent to Grandma. They said they smelled alcohol on her breath at the funeral and she seemed drunk. They want to review the living conditions at the farm. I hate those people. I hate them for what they did to my mother. They never contacted her in all the years I can remember before she died."

"Call me Jim, PerryAnn. Is Grandma drinking?" he asked.

"Yeah, she looked down. She started after Dad and Mom died in the car accident. She wasn't drinking before that. Can you help her stop? I don't want to live in Oklahoma." She finished the last of her pancakes, took the towel Betty handed her and headed to the bathroom for a shower. Ah, it feels good, she thought. The water was hot and she felt the grime from the hours spent on top of the hill slide off her body.

Her thoughts turned to MatiLou. She felt a shiver down her spine. I hope she made it down okay. I hope she won't hate me for leaving her there. The hot water began to turn lukewarm. She turned off the faucet and stepped out of the shower.

As PerryAnn dried off with the towel, the man who picked her up came to her mind. Again, she got a shiver down her spine. Where would she be if he hadn't heard the radio announcement that she was missing? Why was he going down that dirt road? What was that smell on him? She'd seen on television a story about a girl who was kidnapped and held for months as a captive. She couldn't remember the girl's name, but she was her same age. Where was he taking me? She vowed to herself in a whisper, "I will never get into a car with another strange man, and I will never tell anyone that I did today."

Betty knocked on the door. "How is it going in there?" PerryAnn opened the door and came out of the bathroom. Jim Moate was sitting on the couch. "Let's go talk to your grandma."

They took the longer route to the farm because PerryAnn said she wanted to show them where she'd spent the night. What she really wanted was to make sure MatiLou wasn't still there. About thirty miles out of town, they passed the car she'd ridden in with the man. It was pulled way off to the side of the road with wheel locks on the front tires. On the driver side window was a big orange sticker she couldn't read.

When they turned into the parking lot at the foot of the hill, Jim asked, "Are you okay to climb back up there?"

"Sure, she said. It isn't that far. There are stone stairs at the top."

"Betty, are you coming?" Jim asked.

"No, I will wait here."

"Ok, lock the doors and honk the horn if something happens," he said.

PerryAnn and Jim climbed the path and then the stairs to the top of the hill. When they reached the top step, she led the way to the tree where she and MatiLou had put the pack. She called out "hello, hello," but only the sound of her own voice echoed back. She didn't tell Mr. Moate she'd left MatiLou there. "Look over there," he pointed to the trap. "Someone's set a trap. We had better go." PerryAnn couldn't believe her eyes, but inside it was a baby jackrabbit eating the carrots MatiLou had left. The string hadn't worked to close the door. The jackrabbit was free to go when it finished the food.

"I set it," PerryAnn told him and walked over to the trap. She pulled MatiLou's knife out of her pocket, cut the string and removed the door so the jackrabbit couldn't be trapped as it was leaving. She thought MatiLou would be happy to know her trap had worked. She hoped MatiLou would forgive her for leaving her on top of the hill.

Jim Moate and PerryAnn made their way down the hill and back to the car where Betty was waiting. They traveled the road another thirty minutes before they made the turn to the farm. PerryAnn looked up at the sky. The clouds were billowy like they had been thirty hours before when she and MatiLou had left for the park. Jim Moate drove up the drive, past the staked one acre tract, past the rows of cactus to Grandma Waters' house. Spanky, who was sleeping in a chair on the porch, poked his head up as PerryAnn got out of the car and yelled, "Grandma."

The front door opened and the old woman came down the steps. Grandma Waters walked toward PerryAnn and hugged her close. Spanky meowed, jumped down from the chair and rubbed up against PerryAnn's leg. She picked Spanky up and gave him a kiss between his eyes. "Mr. Spanky, I'm so glad to be home."

# CHAPTER SEVEN

My father, mother, and I saw the car and started across the field. PerryAnn looked at me as I walked through the yard. "I'm sorry," she mouthed, but I looked the other way. I hadn't even wanted to go to her grandma's farm when the car with PerryAnn, Jim, and Betty Moate pulled up the drive. My parents made me go.

We all went inside and took seats in Grandma Waters' living room. I sat as far from PerryAnn as I could. I listened to Mr. Moate talk to Grandma Waters about why PerryAnn had come to see him. He asked her if she wanted us to leave, but she said "No, they can stay." He explained to her how PerryAnn told him about her drinking and the letter from child protective services. He explained to her that she could lose PerryAnn if she continued drinking. He said the agency could rule that PerryAnn would have to leave. They could send her to live with her mother's parents in Oklahoma. "Please Grandma, I don't want to go live with them," PerryAnn pleaded.

"I don't drink anymore. I don't have any drinks. Not since I got letter." She looked at PerryAnn. Her eyes filled with tears. "I don't want you to go live in Oklahoma. No more drinks."

As I listened to PerryAnn, I heard her reason for doing what she did. I felt my heart race and my blood seemed hot like it was going to ooze out of me. She explained how she wanted the Moates to help her convince Grandma to stop drinking. She said she'd tried to call, but no one answered the number she dialed. She explained how she hadn't thought of going to find the Moates before we made our trip to the hill, but when she reached the top and saw the way down on the other side and the road connecting her to Albuquerque, she decided to go. I believed everything she said. But I still wondered; if she wasn't planning to go, why did she have their address in her pack?

My mother looked at my father. "We should go."

PerryAnn followed me out of the house. "MatiLou, I have your knife." She handed the red Swiss army knife with MLB engraved on it to me. It was a knife my father had given to me for Christmas. Later, I looked out the window and saw the Moate's car parked in Grandma Waters' drive well into the night.

The next day, I was in the kitchen watching my mother make the pancakes I'd requested when I heard a knock on the front door. On the table was the morning paper with the headline "Sought after drug smuggler captured on county road leading to Albuquerque."

It was PerryAnn at the door. Usually she let herself in, but this morning she knocked. "Can I talk to you?" she asked.

We went outside and sat under the oak tree in the back where my father had added a swing. "MatiLou, I am really sorry. I had to go. I knew you could get down."

I glared at her. "How did you know? Why didn't you wake me up? I asked. "I could have gone with you."

"I'm gonna tell you what happened, but I'm not telling anyone else. You have to promise me you won't say anything," she replied.

"Okay, I promise," I said. I didn't know until PerryAnn told me that she could hear me call her from above and wasn't answering my call. She was looking at the car that was heading toward her that I could not see. "So what happened?" I asked.

"While you were yelling to me a car came down the road and stopped. The man rolled down the window and asked if I needed a ride."

"Yeah," I told him. "I'm going to this address in Albuquerque. Can you take me there?" I showed him the piece of paper with the Moate's address. He opened the door and said, "Sure, get in. I know where that is. I'm heading that way."

"He was skinny and his long, brown hair was tied in a ponytail. He wasn't handsome like the boy in the steel toed boots. He was greasy and smelled of sweat. He had a strange smell I didn't know," she added. "He was gross."

"How old was he?" I asked.

"Twenties, I guess. He told me he'd been up all night working on a drilling rig. I wasn't sure about him, but there wasn't another car in sight. I was determined to get to Albuquerque, so I got in. Anyway, I was afraid I might give in to your calls from the top of the hill. I didn't want to lose my chance to go."

"Why didn't you wake me up?" I asked again. "I could have gone with you!"

"It was something I had to do myself. I was afraid you would try to stop me. I knew you could get down or I wouldn't have left you there." We sat in silence for several minutes. "I had a really scary encounter. I wasn't going to tell anyone, but I want to tell you. Promise me again you'll keep it a secret."

I nodded agreement with her request.

"He started down a dirt road," she continued. But when he heard the announcement on the radio that I was missing, he backed up and dropped me on the main road. The scary thing is that when I got in the car, I looked down and he had on dirty cowboy boots like the ones I told you about in my dream. Remember the dream I told you about? It was so weird that he heard the announcement when he did. If he hadn't, I don't know where I would be. It was like someone was watching over me." She went on. The Moates and I passed his car on the way here. It was at the side of the road with wheel locks and an orange sticker on the window."

"I think he was caught. It was in the paper," I said. I thought it was dumb of her to get in the car with the man. I would never do something like that. Well, when I thought about it, I actually had on that very same day. I'd gotten in

134

the truck at the parking lot with both the bikes and let the man I didn't know drive me to the gate at the park entrance. I didn't know him anymore than she knew the man who picked her up on the road. It was dumb of both of us really.

We sat in silence again. I felt the knot that had been in my stomach ever since we started our journey yesterday begin to dissolve. "Hey, I almost forgot," PerryAnn said. We went back up the hill on the way here. Mr. Moate wanted to see where we'd been stranded, but I wanted to check to see if you were still there. Your trap had a baby jackrabbit in it. The trap door hadn't sprung, but it was in there eating the carrots you left."

"Wow, it worked. I'm so excited. I'll have to figure out a way to get my dad to go up there with me so I can see for myself. There isn't too much food in the trap, so we will have to go tomorrow." I was feeling frantic. I sure didn't want that baby jackrabbit to be harmed by my trap.

"No need to go back. I cut the string with your knife, so it wouldn't get trapped by the door spring releasing on the way out. I figured you wouldn't mind."

"Oh, thank you!" *My dad will never have to know.* I gave her a big hug and kissed her cheek. It was then I knew I was no longer mad at her for leaving me on the hill.

When we returned to the house and devoured the pancakes my mother left warming on stove, the paper was still lying on the table. We read the article about the man who'd picked PerryAnn up. He'd been caught because he was traveling twenty miles over the speed limit. The policeman who'd stopped him ran his tag and found there was a warrant for his arrest. He had a record for manufacturing and selling illegal drugs. There was no mention of PerryAnn in the article. She said that because she got into the car with him and they mentioned her as missing on the radio, he'd been caught. "In a weird way, I feel good for that, but I'll never get in a car with a strange man again. I learned my lesson," she said.

I shuddered as she spoke. I thought of the man she had described. One of the darkest moments of my life could have been the morning I awoke from a dream where I was an Indian Princess and found PerryAnn was gone.

The summer of 1973 was a time filled with incredible change, for PerryAnn and for me. We would never be the same.

PerryAnn and I are still close friends even though I no longer see her in the same way I did before we made our journey to the hill. She left the farm after her senior year and lives with the Moates in Albuquerque while she attends junior college for her legal assistant associate degree. The money Grandma Waters took for the sale of her minerals is helping to pay for her degree. She says she plans to return to the farm next year to help Grandma Waters with her cactus growing and to help Jim Moate with *Natives for Nature*. She says she hasn't seen the boy with the steel toed boots again, and her mother's parents continue to try to connect with her. She says she's still too mad at how they treated her mother to have anything to do with them. She still plans to investigate her parents' accident when she returns to the farm.

I left last summer after my senior year to attend college in Albuquerque. I am studying to be a wildlife biologist and wrote this novella about our summer in 1973 for my English writing assignment. The truth I discovered in writing it is that I found an inner strength from coming down the hill alone.

Grandma Waters has continued to stay away from drinking, and although she won't say she is an alcoholic, once or twice a week she goes to town for an AA meeting or two. My father says she has continued to make a small living growing and selling her cacti plants. He has continued studying rocks of New Mexico, and is writing a book on the subject. His rock shop on our farm continues to draw rock hunters, tourists, and just about anyone passing by on the road. The sign between the farms reads Grandma Waters' Cactus Farm with an arrow pointing left and Rocks of New Mexico with an arrow pointing right. In small print are the words 'organic vegetables and bunnies for sale.'

My mother has continued to paint and was recognized as a top New Mexico landscape artist last year. People from all over the state are commissioning her work. After the scare of my night on the hill, she and I connected in a stronger way than we ever had before, and I don't think she's called me Matilda Louise once since that day.

The park added a gate, which would close the road, so if a ranger isn't there, you cannot pass through. No one has been in the park unaccounted for at night as far as anyone knows since we spent the night on the top of the hill.

The man who picked PerryAnn up on the road to Albuquerque was sentenced to prison for selling drugs. She called the prison to find out when he'd be released and found out he was killed in a gang fight last year.

Dirk died in a barroom fight. The drilling activity stopped abruptly three months after he came to stake the one acre tract on Grandma Waters' farm. The tract still sits there as a reminder of a looming threat. A well could one day be drilled on her farm because she sold the minerals without discussing it with anyone on that hot summer day in 1973.